Folens Primary Art

Picture Pack
Art of Different Cultures

Key Stage 2

Folens
Publishers

Elaine Baker

Acknowledgements

The author and publishers would like to thank the Trustees of the British Museum for permission to reproduce all the photographs in this pack.

The art objects under discussion in this pack are all to be found in the Museum of Mankind, London.

ISBN 1 85276487-2

Illustrations by Elaine Baker.
Cover by Gordon Davies of Moss Davies Dandy Turner Ltd.

First published 1992 by Folens Limited, Dunstable and Dublin.
Folens Limited, Albert House, Apex Business Centre, Boscombe Road, Dunstable, LU5 4RL, England.

Printed in Great Britain by Kenley Press, Dunstable.

Contents

Time Line

1450 Bornu dynasty begins to rise.
Bronze casting is brought to Benin from Ife.
Ewuare the Great is King of the Benin.
Joã d'Aveiro visits Benin.

1600 The Songhai peoples are overthrown by the Moroccan armies in the Sudan which upsets the Sahara trade patterns.
Portuguese, English and Dutch traders visit Benin.
The State of Oyo reaches the zenith of its power.
Kilwa is destroyed by the Zimba people.
King Osei Tuti unites the weak forest states making the Ashanti tribe dominant over their neighbours.
Kongo peoples and kingdom disintegrate after the anti-slavery wars.

A Benin Mask, ivory and copper pectoral mask.
South Nigeria, Africa, 16th Century.
Museum of Mankind , London.

QUESTIONS ?

1. The citizens of Benin stopped work and enjoyed a day or more of festivities every month. They would drink bamboo wine, play games, dance and chew kola nuts.
Their festivities sound similar to many still occurring round the world. They chewed kola nuts as a stimulant; we have a drink containing the same ingredients but spelled slightly differently. What is it?

2. Do you like the pectoral mask? Can you explain why?

3. How would you compare this with the American Indian mask? (Picture 9.)
Discuss the differences and any similarities.

4. Which of the two do you prefer and why?

5. Why do you think ivory and copper were kept solely for use by the royal family? Do you think that they thought of conservation then?

TECHNIQUES

The mask is exquisitely carved from ivory and then inlaid with copper wire. The craftsmen of Benin were renowned for their fine work and this is one the of most beautiful examples of it.
Ivory and copper were materials kept exclusively for royal use.

ACTIVITIES

Individuals

1. This mask is a beautifully crafted object. Draw it as carefully as you can, putting in as much detail as possible.

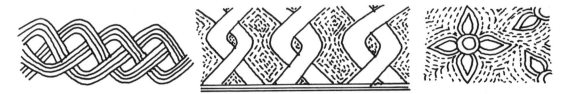

2. Benin was a bustling commercial centre that traded throughout Western Africa, dealing in weapons, tools, ironwork, wood carvings and foodstuffs. They also had a currency consisting of cowrie shells and metal rings called manillas.
   Design a poster for the market-place advertising their wares and giving prices. Compare it with present-day advertising.

In Small Groups

3. The King and Queen Hother wore elaborate collars and head coverings. The King also carried a decorative sword like the one on the right. It is totally different from European swords. This was not intended as a weapon, more a symbol of power.
   Design a symbol of power suitable for a king or ruler; think carefully of the symbols you could use.

4. The artists of Benin used many varied patterns, both as a background to their work and as decoration.
   Make a design using the Benin patterns.

Background

A BENIN MASK

This is a very famous pectoral mask made from ivory and copper. It is dated around the 16th Century and comes from Benin in south Nigeria, Africa.
The King of this tribe was called the Oba, and this would have been worn by him at the festival of Ugie Iye Oba held to commemorate his dead mother.
This mask is thought to depict the Queen Mother Idia, a very powerful figure and the mother of the Oba, Esigie.

The marks above the eyes represent the raised scars worn by high-ranking women, and the tiara of little Portuguese heads is intended to suggest the power and wealth of the royal house which had the monopoly of foreign trade.

Time Line

1450	BENIN	- Ewuare the Great is King.
	CONGO	- Congo is founded by Bakobngo warriors.
	KILWA	- The Portuguese fleet arrives with Pedro Cabral.
	ZIMBABWE	- Neighbouring tribes conquered by King Mutota.
1500	BENIN	- Joã d'Aveiro visits Benin.
	CONGO	- The Portuguese reach the Congo river.
	KILWA	- Kilwa is sacked by the Portuguese.
1600	BENIN	- Benin visited by Portuguese, English and Dutch traders.
	YORUBA	- Oyo state reaches the peak of its power.
	CONGO	- Congo disintegrates following anti-slavery wars.
1750	YORUBA	- Yoruba peoples divided and weakened by slave raids.
	ZIMBABWE	- Zimbabwe overrun by Nguni tribesmen.
1900		The British annexe Benin and Yoruba. The Belgians annexe Congo.

QUESTIONS ? ? ? ? ? ? ? ? ?

1. Why do you think they hold fans? Could it be because of the heat or as a symbol of royalty?

2. The chief has two wives and one child. Which wife will be the child's mother? Why?

3. Could the brazier and bowl be there to show that the chief is hungry or could there be other reasons?

4. Do you like this group? Why?

5. They are going to a festival, why do you think that they are dressed in their best clothes?

TECHNIQUES

This group is modelled from clay and fired with a glaze. There is careful modelling of the faces and the fans with patterned detail added.

Background

A KWALE IBO POTTERY GROUP

This is a pottery group of figures on a stand used in the Yam cult among the Kwale Ibo tribe of Osisa village in Nigeria.

It represents a family group consisting of a chief in the centre, holding a horn and a fan, with a wife on either side of him holding fans. The wife on the right is also holding a child. There is a seated attendant in front of them holding a gong, and on the ground before the group are a brazier and a bowl.

ACTIVITIES

Individuals

1. Look carefully at the group and draw just one small part. Put in as much detail as possible and try to shade darker areas.

2. Paint your own family group. Try to group them closely together and place the youngest in the front.

3. Look at the patterns on this and compare them with the Benin ivory mask.
   Make a design from these with a 15 cm square. Use only brown, black and white.

In Small Groups

4. Working in pairs make clay figures for a family group. Each pair can make one figure. Therefore four pairs will produce four figures to place on the decorated stand made by the last pair.
   They will also need to provide bowls, etc. to place on the stand with the figures.

Group or Whole Class

5. Here is a plan of an African village. The inward facing huts have raised, circular doorways to keep out domestic animals and rodents. Draw out the plan of a village and build it. Domestic animals could be put in the courtyard and much detail used in stocking the huts with pots, etc.

Older Boys' Hut
Storage Pots
Granary

Husband's Hut

Wife's Hut
Grindstone
Storage Pots

Younger Children's Hut
Granary

Older Girls' Hut
Granary
Grindstone

A Kwale Ibo. *Yam Festival Pottery Group, 46 cm high. Museum of Mankind, London.*

Time Line

1500 BC	The climate of the Sahara becomes drier. Horses which have been domesticated are introduced from Egypt.
500 BC	The Sahara becomes too dry for horses, camels are introduced. Men abandon the desert and settlements decline.
AD 1000	The Sahara is overrun by Moslem Arabs from the Near East.
1150	Moslem merchants begin to settle in North African cities.
1450	Songhai absorbs the state of Mali.
1600	Songhai overthrown by Moslem armies, this upsets the Sahara trade patterns.
1900	Western Sudan is occupied by France.

A Skin Vessel *from northern Nigeria made by the Tuareg people.*
Museum of Mankind, London.

QUESTIONS?? ?

1. What do you think these loops or handles would have been used for?

2. What would this vessel have been used to hold?

3. Camel trains transported goods across the Sahara and in the north items were then moved by donkey trains, but when items were sent south, donkeys were not always suitable means of transport and there were no roads, only tracks.
   How do you think goods were transported at this time?

4. Camels can be bad tempered and nasty animals and are not easy to control. What would it have been like to be in charge of a camel train?

5. How would you stop your camel wandering off at night?
   Remember there would be no trees or anything to tie it to.

TECHNIQUES

Skin or hide vessels are of particular use to travellers. They were not so easy to break as pottery and would help to keep liquids cool. The Tuareg, who made them, were a travelling people navigating the Sahara by sun, stars and the wind patterns in the sand. These are reflected in the design.

ACTIVITIES

Individuals

1. Look carefully at the picture and draw the patterns that you can see. Colour them in using black and white.

2. Use either white cut paper on a black background or vice versa, and make a repeating pattern from the work previously drawn suitable for printing.
If possible make a block or use a screen and print the design.

In Small Groups

3. Another form of popular patterned fabric is tie and dye. Small clean pebbles or dried peas are placed on clean cotton fabric and the cloth gathered and tied tightly around them. 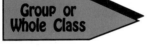 (It can be a random design or a carefully structured one.) The cloth is then dyed, string and pebbles removed and it is dried and pressed. A second tying and dying in a different colour can be done. This technique lends itself to great experimentation.

4. Using a coiled pot technique, build a clay pot similar in shape to the picture.
Decorate in a similar style.

Group or Whole Class

5. Put all the work together in a large display. Some sand, models of camels, an oasis, models of square tiny windowed houses, and palm trees would be an appropriate background for the vessels and their decoration.

Background

AN AFRICAN SKIN VESSEL

This African vessel was made by the Tuareg tribe of northern Nigeria, possibly from the Sokoto area.
The bottle is made of treated animal skin, with small handles on the bowl and decorative loops at the top.
It is ornately patterned.

Picture 4

Time Line

1526	New Guinea visited by Dorn Jorge de' Meneses. (It is thought that the natives resembled those of West Africa.)
1605-56	New Guinea visited by Dutch explorers including Abel Tasman.
1700-1800	Various explorers, including Sampier and James Cook, visited the coasts but very little knowledge was gained of the country or its people.
1800-1900	Explorers and scientific observers visited; some of these were sponsored by various European governments, notably the Dutch. Areas of New Guinea and the islands surrounding it were annexed by the British, Dutch and Germans. After the end of World War I, the territory of New Guinea was passed to Australia under mandate from the League of Nations.

QUESTIONS????????

1. What do you think would be frightening about this?

2. Why would this be a difficult mask to wear? What problems do you think it would cause for the wearer?

3. Would you like to wear it?

4. What type of costume do you think would have been worn with it?

5. What occasions would you wear a mask for? A funeral? Maybe a party? Can you think of any other times?

A Carved Wooden Malangan Mask,
New Ireland province, Papua New Guinea.
Museum of Mankind, London.

ACTIVITIES

Individuals

In Small Groups

Group or Whole Class

1. Look carefully at the patterns on the mask. Use them to make a design.

2. From the design made previously, make a printing block either from press print, lino, screen or potato and print on to paper or cloth.
   Use the design as a repeating pattern.
   Fabric could be printed to use as drapes for display.

3. Use the patterns produced previously and put them on to claywork, either as a pattern on a thumb or coil pot, or as a raised pattern on a tile.

4. Use cardboard, plastic, and found materials or wire and papier mâché and make masks. Decorate them in an appropriate manner and then discuss their use apart from decoration.
   A ceremony could be organised with music (percussive) written by the children in which the masks could be used. This would involve collaboration of music, dance, art and drama.

TECHNIQUES

The mask is made from carved wood which has been traditionally decorated in brown and white. It is horned and has shaped guards across the face.

Background

A MALANGAN MASK

Masks from Papua New Guinea, were carved and formed from wood. These were mainly used in the course of funerary rites. It was believed that they were the temporary containers for the spirits of the dead people, waiting to be re-channelled back to the living world.

Picture 5

1st Century AD	Java was visited by the Hindus, firstly as traders and later bringing priests. The Hindus intermarried with the Javanese and spread their religion and culture.
1500	When the Portuguese visited Java in the 16th Century, they found, "The most civilised people in these parts". Islam is introduced into Java, and gradually the Javanese became Moslems.
1596	The first Dutch traders visited Java.
1602	The formation of the Dutch East India Company.
1800	At the end of the Napoleonic period France laid claim to the Eastern Dutch possessions; this brought in the British who defeated the French at Weltervereden.
1811	Stamford Raffles was appointed Lieutenant Governor. He revolutionised the administrative system, abolished the system of tributes and introduced reforms to the land and legal systems. He was in charge until 1816 when he returned the islands to the Dutch. This gamelan was one of the Javanese artefacts that he brought back to Britain.

QUESTIONS????????

1. This is a musical instrument. What modern instrument does it remind you of?

2. The keys are bronze suspended over bamboo resonators. What sort of sound do you think it would make?

3. What do you like about the decoration on the front?

4. What is is about these colours that make it look impressive and suitable for the royal court orchestra?

5. Do you think that it would be moved around or would it be rather heavy?

Background

THE "RAFFLES" GAMELAN

This is a musical instrument from Indonesia, a gender with bronze keys. The gender is one of the main parts of the traditional Indonesian court gamelan orchestra.

This is a particularly tall example resembling earlier examples from the 15th and 16th Centuries.
A gamelan is looked upon as a manifestation of a special supernatural power and gamelan music is played for both secular and religious meetings.
The musicians play as a group, therefore there is little scope for individual ideas and interpretation.

TECHNIQUES

This is a musical instrument that would be used within the traditional court "gamelan" orchestra. It is made of wood, painted and decorated in red, gold and black. The keys are suspended on strings above vertical bamboo resonators.

ACTIVITIES

Individuals

1. Draw and paint the creature on the front of the gamelan. Look particularly at the head and the style which is typical of Indonesian art.

2. Use the different patterns found on this and with just three colours produce an abstract design.

In Small Groups

3. Make this creature either from clay or from card and then write a short story about it.

Group or Whole Class

4. Discuss the types of musical instrument which may have been played with the gamelan, i.e. flute, drum, cymbals, rattles, etc. Make some of these from beads, wood, plastic, paper, in fact anything that would be suitable.
   When the instruments have been produced which make sounds, then a piece or pieces of music can be written in conjunction with the music specialist and performed.

The "Raffles" Gamelan, *Java, Indonesia late 18th or early 19th Century.*
The Museum of Mankind, London.

13

Picture 6

Time Line

13th C	Java was referred to by Marco Polo in his writings. It was a mainly Hindu area.
1293-1520	The rise of the kingdom of Majapahit; after the overthrow of this kingdom Java was split into many kingdoms or provinces. Islam was introduced to Java by traders from Malacca, Sumatra and Giyarat. Gradually the Javanese became Moslems.
1596	The first Dutch traders visited Java.
1602	The formation of the Dutch East India Company.
1610	A Governor General is appointed and the Dutch gradually extended their power and holdings in the island.
1800	At the end of the Napoleonic period, France laid claim to Dutch possessions in the East. The British fought and defeated the French at Weltervereden.
1811	Stamford Raffles was appointed Lieutenant Governor.
1816	Java was returned to the Dutch. Gradually the Indonesians were given more independence.
1942	Indonesia was invaded by the Japanese.
1945-6	The Japanese were defeated and abandoned possession of the islands.

A Shadow Puppet *of Laksamana made of hide,
Java, Indonesia.
Museum of Mankind, London.*

QUESTIONS ? ? ? ? ? ? ? ?

1. Make a shadow puppet.
   You don't need any tools, only your hands in front of a light source to cast a shadow on a wall.

2. These puppets would have been used to tell stories, often to people who could not read. Can you name famous husband and wife puppets? (Normally you would see them at the seaside.)

3. Shadow puppets are not the only type of puppet. There are also glove puppets, marionettes (string puppets), rod puppets, paper bag puppets, and sock puppets.
   What would it be like to play with any of these?

4. What part of the decoration of these puppets is particularly noticeable?

ACTIVITIES

Individuals

1. Carefully draw a silhouette of this Wayang (shadow puppet). Try to put in all the detail you can see.

2. Design a poster to advertise a puppet play. You will need the title of the play, time of performance, place, price and any other information. Only use three colours and make sure that the poster is eye-catching.

In Small Groups

3. These next activities will form part of a whole performance.
   - Design and construct a puppet theatre.
     (Wood and corrugated card would be a useful start.)
   - Design and make six puppet characters:
     Hero
     Villain
     Villain's assistant
     Heroine
     Clown or Hero's friend
     Animal.

   - Write a play for these characters.
   - Design and make the scenery for the play.
   - Rehearse and perform it.

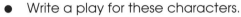

TECHNIQUES

This is a typical Wayang puppet made for a Javanese shadow show. It is intricately made and carved from stiff hide. Limbs would be hinged and moved with fine rods. The puppet would be backlit against a screen so that the puppeteer below would not be seen.

Background

A SHADOW PUPPET - WAYANG

Shadow puppets like these from Indonesia help to act out the story of the Ramayana. Rama won the hand of the beautiful Sita by bending and stringing the bow of Shiva.

Rama and Sita were exiled to the forests for fourteen years and were accompanied by Rama's brother, Laksamana. They were eventually rescued with the help of the King of the Monkeys.

Puppetry has been an important form of entertainment in the Far East for centuries and the puppets are both intricate and beautiful works of art.

Both rod and shadow puppets are popular in Java and the puppeteers are among the most skilful. These puppets are now much sought after.

Time Line

1567 Islands are discovered by Spaniard Alraro Mendaria and named Islas de Solomon.
He surveyed the three large islands to the south of the group and named them San Cristoval, Guadalcanal and Ysabel.

1768 Louis de Bougainville discovered the three northern islands (Buka, Choiseul and Boufarville).

1845 Major Epaulle, the first vicar apostolic of Melanesia, was killed by the natives.

1920 The League of Nations assigned the islands to Australia.

1942 The Japanese seized the Solomon Islands during World War II and built a strategically important airfield on Guadalcanal island.
October 25-26th. A severe battle fought with the Americans who lost an aircraft carrier and destroyer. The Japanese lost two carriers, two battleships, three cruisers and one hundred aeroplanes.
November 13-15th. Another battle in which the Japanese lost a battleship, three heavy cruisers, two light cruisers, five destroyers and eight transporters with thirty thousand soldiers aboard. American losses were two light cruisers and six destroyers.

QUESTIONS ? ? ? ? ? ? ? ? ? ?

1. Look at the small shield and find the outline of a human face.

2. Look at the shields of the warriors on the Mexican Codex. How do they differ from these?

3. Which do you think would be most effective in battle?

4. The Solomon Islands were famous for their large canoes with striking bow carvings. This is a drawing of one. They were believed to protect the canoe and sailors from danger. Can you think of other types of sailing vessels that had carved figures on the bow?

Background

SOLOMON ISLAND SHIELDS

The larger shield is made from wicker with a stylised human figure and patterns marked out in pearl shell.
The smaller shield is older and is made from a flat piece of wood 2 mm thick which has been bent backwards into a curve. Along the centre of the back is a rattan handle (decorated with carving). The front of the shield is painted with a fretwork pattern in black and red, the outline of which is formed by small strips of mother-of-pearl shell.
At one end of the shield is the outline of a human face.
The whole surface of the shield has been smeared with gum before painting to give it a smooth surface.

TECHNIQUES

The larger shield is made of wicker, vegetable resin and pearl shell.
The smaller shield is made of wood, rattan, cane, hair, pearl shell and gum.

ACTIVITIES

Individuals

1. Carefully draw the larger shield and paint the design in black and white.

2. Look carefully at the smaller shield. The design could be composed of interlocking letters. Use a letter of the alphabet either A, E, F, H, K, M, N, W, or Z and make a pattern from this. Colour it in only red, black and white.

In Small Groups

3. Now take three letters from the ones above and with an oval shield shape make a design. It would be very effective to cut the letters out from white paper and glue them to a black background. It also opens up the possibilities of moving patterns around until a suitable one is decided upon.

4. Make larger designs in red, black and white using the pictorial and design elements of these shields with a patterned border. Use small squares of paper and stick them into place as the mother-of-pearl would have been fixed into the original shields.

5. Fruit, vegetables and fish would have been the main diet of the islanders. Make mobiles of their foodstuffs. Colour the designs in brown, white, red and black and suspend them. Use small squares to decorate them.

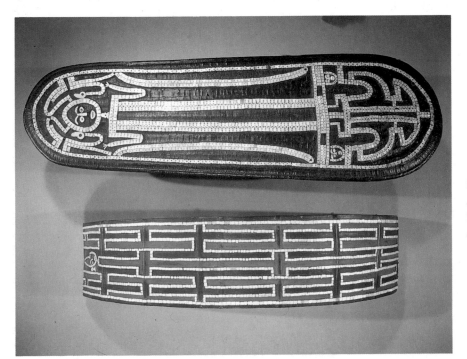

Shields *from the Solomon Islands. The smaller shield is approximately 92 cm in length. Museum of Mankind, London.*

Picture 8

Time Line

AD 1000	Indian priests came to Tibet and revived Buddhism.
1100-1200	The priests steadily increased their power.
1358	Priestly discipline had become very lax and reforms were urgently needed. These were brought about by a religious reformer named Tsong Ka-pa. Tsong Ka-pa's successor was called Gan-den Trup-pa and when he died in 1474 his spirit was believed to have entered a baby boy born two years later. This child became his successor and thus began the system of priestly incarnation.
1700	The Chinese sought to increase their power in Tibet.
1788	The Ghurkas from Nepal invaded Tibet but were defeated by a mixed force of Chinese and Tibetans.
1800	Europeans were prevented from entering Tibet.
1904	A British Expedition reached Llasa.
1911	The Chinese Revolution erupted in China enabling the Tibetans to drive out the now disorganised Chinese army.
1922	Llasa was linked to India by telegraph.
1940	Chinese and Tibetan relations improved and the new Dalai Lama was enthroned on 22nd February.
1965	The Chinese declared Tibet an Autonomous Region of China. Since then approximately 85 000 Tibetans are believed to have left and some 500 000 Chinese have moved in and settled there.

QUESTIONS ? ? ? ? ? ? ? ?

1. Who, or what, is a Tibetan Lama?

2. This silk dancing dress would have belonged to a wealthy person. When do you think it was worn?

3. Describe the patterns on the robe? Do you like them?

4. Use an atlas to find out the name of Tibet's capital city.

5. Tibet is the source of many important rivers, and mountains. Use an atlas to name three large rivers that start in Tibet and name the three highest mountains.

A Lama's Silk Dancing Dress, *various colours with brocade. Museum of Mankind, London.*

TECHNIQUES

A woven silk brocade robe. This is embroidered and decorated with tinsel, satin and silk.
The colourful decorations depict dragons.

ACTIVITIES

Individuals

1. Look carefully at the patterns on the sleeves and design a panel using these shapes and colours.

2. The dragon was the sacred symbol of the East, the rain spirit (Gatherer of the Clouds).
   Take just the head of the dragon but enlarge it. Use different coloured papers and textures and make a lively collage.

In Small Groups

3. Make a decorated dragon kite. These are just a few shapes to consider. Decorate the dragon kite and remember to give him a tail.

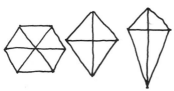

Group or Whole Class

4. Using the word **Dragons**, decorate the separate letters with fanciful dragons.
   Each group can work on one large letter. This could be done in a variety of materials dependent on their availability, e.g. fabrics, clay, paint, found materials.

5. Make dragon puppets (a rod puppet would be the most suitable). This could be made on a large scale like the Chinese New Year dragons if wanted.

Background

A LAMA'S SILK DANCING DRESS

This brocade robe made for a Lama in Tibet is made from silk and is decorated with silks, satin and tinsel. The colourful decoration depicts a dragon. It would have been worn for dancing. There is much Chinese influence in this garment, both in the fabric that has been used and the decoration. This garment would have been worn in the summer as winters were cold and cloth lined with lambskin was worn then. The robe would have reached to the ankle. Earrings were universally worn and the official earring has a standard pattern, being long and narrow and hanging from a gold ring set with a pearl. It was worn in the left ear.

Picture 9

Time Line

AD 1400 — Incas navigate South American coasts.

1492 — Christopher Columbus reaches America.

1500 — John Cabot lands at Newfoundland and claims the land for England.
The Inca and Aztec empires are conquered by Spain and the Indians are reduced to slavery.
Negro slaves are brought from Africa to the West Indies. France, Holland and England discover and explore America.
The French begin an exploration of the St. Lawrence Valley.

1600-1800 — Holland, France and England begin settlement of the North American continent.
Settlers meet opposition from native Indians.

1800 — Many of the Indian tribes were defeated and wiped out in the Indian wars.
Others were granted land from the Government called "reservations".
They carry on many of the artistic traditions of their ancestors.

QUESTIONS ? ? ? ? ? ? ? ? ?

1. How is this mask made to look fierce?

2. Which animals or birds do you think are represented on the mask?

3. Look at the sketch of the side view of this mask. Do you think that this would have been worn or would it have been fixed to a building? What facts make you reach your decision?

4. Why do you think the small animal heads seem to be listening to the larger one?
Do you think that the large head is the most important one?

5. Write a short conversation between the different heads on the mask. It might be an argument as to who is the most important and why. Now act out the conversation with friends.

TECHNIQUES

The mask is cut and carved from solid pale wood in the form of a human face with a bird's beak. The mask is painted in green, black and red.

A Wooden Mask.
North American Indian, possibly Haida.
27cm high x 24.5cm wide.
Museum of Mankind, London.

ACTIVITIES

Individuals

1. Look carefully at the patterns on this mask. Design a mask based on the picture and use only red, black, yellow and green to decorate it.

2. Indian tribes all over North America believed in a great spirit called the Thunderbird. He is huge and sends thunder from his great wings, lightning from his flashing eyes and water from the great pool he carries on his back.
Design and cut out from cardboard a Thunderbird. Decorate the shapes and suspend them on cords. Design cloud and lightning symbols to suspend with the Thunderbirds.

3. Make a clay mask in the same style as this one. Build up the shapes as three-dimensional patterns. Colour in the same colours as the picture.

In Small Groups

4. The Indians used buffalo hide for many things, one of which was a parfleche, a large envelope-shaped carrier for their meat or clothes. From the pattern given at the back of this book make a parfleche from stiff card to carry some of your papers or a book.

Group or Whole Class

5. Assemble a collection of boxes, and in small groups decorate each box into part of a totem pole with a face on each side. Assemble the boxes into a totem pole. Don't forget to put the Thunderbird on the top.

Background

A WOODEN MASK

This grotesque mask from the North-west coast of America has been cut from solid pale wood to resemble a human face but with a bird's beak. It has five animal-faced heads of graduated sizes fixed around the edge. These are fixed by means of tongs sliding into the mask. The ears on the side figures incline towards the central one as though they are listening. There are two small arms fixed to the bottom of the mask and it is painted in green, black and red.

This mask comes probably from the Haida tribe, who were known for the beautifully carved and decorated totem poles, dug-out canoes and masks that they made.

This is a side view of the mask.

Time Line

600 BC	Monte Alban is built probably by the Zapotecs. This is a major ceremonial centre.
300	Major temples are built and Monte Alban develops.
AD 900	The ceremonial centre Monte Alban is abandoned.
1000	Toltecs overpower many of the small independent states. Mixtec peoples expand. Chief Eight Deer Ocelot Claw is the ruler.
1200	Mixtecs use Monte Alban for royal burials. In Europe Marco Polo journeys to China.
1300	City states compete for power throughout Mexico. The Black Death sweeps through Europe.
1400	The Aztecs try to conquer the Mixtecs and Zapotecs - they are unsuccessful. In Europe Joan of Arc leads the armies of France against England. Gutenberg invents the printing press. The Italian Renaissance reaches its height.
1492	Christopher Columbus discovers America.
1500	Cortés lands in Mexico and conquers the different tribes. Spanish settlers arrive and take away the wealth and land from the Indians.

QUESTIONS ? ? ? ? ? ? ? ?

1. When one man is drawn bigger than another, it shows that he is more important. Can you find any important men in this picture?

2. The Aztecs did not use words in this picture. If we are drawing cartoons we use speech balloons. To show that someone is speaking the Aztecs drew blue scrolls coming out of their mouths. Can you find anyone who is speaking in the picture?

3. If the Aztecs wanted to show that something was further away, they drew it near the top of the page, and if someone was travelling it was shown by a line of footprints on a page. Find either of these things on this picture.

4. Warriors have shields and weapons. How many are there?

Background

THE NUTTAL CODEX

Codex is the European name for an Aztec manuscript. This particular manuscript is believed to have been sent from Mexico with the Codex Vienna by Cortés to Charles V, King of Spain, in 1519.

It was in the possession of the Dominican Monastery of San Marco, Florence, Italy in 1859. It was then sold to John Temple Leader.

After this it came into the possession of Robert Curzon, 14th Baron Zouche, and was acquired by the British Museum in 1917.

The Codex gives the history and family background of one of the Mixtec rulers, Eight Deer.

TECHNIQUES

This codex predicts the Spanish conquest of Mexico. It is a deer skin screenfold painted on both sides; there are forty-seven leaves each 19 cm x 25.5 cm.

The codex was folded like a concertina and both sides were used to tell the story or give information. In this case the story is of Eight Deer and four of his early military victories.

ACTIVITIES

Individuals

1. Choose a small part of the Codex and carefully draw it. Look at it and try to write your interpretation of this part of the story.

2. Chief Eight Deer is represented by a buck's head and eight circles. He greatly expanded his realm through strategic marriage, conquests and the sacrifice of his potential rivals to the gods.
Look at the pictographs and draw the ones that represent names. Place them in a long border design that can be folded like a codex.

In Small Groups

3. The war shields were decorated with feathers. Make cardboard circular war shields but instead of feathers use overlapping tissue shapes to represent feathers.

4. Make models of a temple. What materials could be used? Both small and larger models could be made and put together into a small city.

Group or Whole Class

5. Assemble all the different pieces of work made. The name pictographs could be used for a border and all this work could be displayed with that based on the turquoise mosaic serpent (picture 11) to make a display.

A Page from the Nuttal Codex.
Mexico - Mixtec.
Museum of Mankind, London.

Picture 11

Time Line

AD 1100	The Aztecs move in to the Valley of Mexico upon the downfall of the Toltec empire. In Europe the establishment of universities in Paris and Oxford. Thomas à Becket is murdered in Canterbury Cathedral. The Inca civilisation grows and builds huge stone fortresses.
1200	City States in competition for power throughout Mexico. In Europe the Magna Carta is signed. Mongols invade Hungary and Poland.
1300	The Aztec capital Tenochtitlan is built. In Europe the Hundred Years War begins between France and England. Europe is swept by the Black Death. In England the Peasants' Revolt is suppressed.
1400	Aztec armies conquer territories in southern Mexico. A great empire is built and Montezuma I is elected as their Chief Speaker. The temple at Tenochtitlan is dedicated and 20 000 victims are sacrificed. In Europe Italian Renaissance reaches its height.
1492	Christopher Columbus discovers America.
1500	Montezuma II becomes ruler of the Aztecs.
1521	Cortés lands at Vera Cruz and conquers Tenochtitlan with the aid of enemy tribes. Montezuma is killed and the Aztec empire is destroyed. In Europe the Spanish Armada is destroyed by the English fleet. Holland and England reach the Americas. The French land in Canada.
1580	Drake circumnavigates the world.

QUESTIONS

1. Think of how this ornament was made. Do you think that it would be light or heavy to wear?

2. One of the Aztec Gods was called "The Feathered Serpent". Can you find its name?

3. Why do you think this ornament was made with a plain hollow wooden back?

4. Do you like this ornament? Do you think the serpent heads look fierce?

5. The Aztecs did not use money, they had a barter system and cocoa beans were used as small change to even out any differences in value.
They used beans because they were easy to carry and everyone liked cocoa.
Discuss the idea of barter today. Could it work in a small community like a school and what could you use as small change?

Background

AN AZTEC TURQUOISE PECTORAL ORNAMENT

This turquoise mosaic serpent from Mexico is made from wood, turquoise and shell. This is a chest ornament in the form of a double-headed serpent 43 cm long.

This would have been worn by a member of the Aztec nobility, as the semi-precious stone turquoise was regarded as being sacred, and was worn to denote rank.

As well as chest ornaments a warrior or one of the nobility would also wear ear plugs, a nose plug and a lip plug. There were very strict laws about the wearing of jewellery. For instance, a man wearing a crystal nose plug when he was not entitled to wear it could be punished by death.

This piece of turquoise jewellery was purchased from the Duchessa Massino through Lord Washington with £100 from the Christy Fund in September 1894.

24

ACTIVITIES

Individuals

1. The Aztecs used face stamps (a form of painted tattoo). These are two examples of the type of design they used.
   Design a face stamp based either on a bird or a circular shape. Use just one colour on white.

2. You would have found Aztec food rather different. The peasants ate mainly maize and beans. The only domestic animals were turkeys, dogs and rabbits which were kept and fattened for special occasions. They had steamed pancakes stuffed with fish, cactus, worms or tadpoles and they ate tortillas, grilled then dipped in hot pepper and tomatoes. Design a menu for an Aztec meal. Use a border design which includes the different foods.

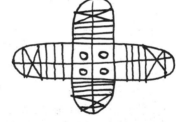

In Small Groups

3. Design a chest ornament based on an animal or reptile.

4. The Aztecs played a game called "Patolli" for four players. The mat had fifty-two squares. It was played with red and blue counters and dice rather like lotto. The player won when he had three counters in a row. Discuss how many counters are needed each and make a set of rules and a board. Now play the game.

TECHNIQUES

This pectoral ornament of a double-headed serpent is of red wood completely covered on the front with turquoise mosaic. Details of the mouths and gums are covered in red shell and the teeth in white shell. The eye sockets are now empty but probably contained shell or iron pyrites. Both serpent heads are entirely covered with mosaics but the body is covered on the front only.

Aztec Turquoise Pectoral Ornament.
43 cm long x 20 cm high.
Museum of Mankind, London.

Time Line

AD 300	Geographers in the Western World believed that a great southern continent existed. They named it Terra Australita Incognita (the unknown southern continent).
1600	Dutch explorers, among them Abel Tasman, Van Diemen and Van Hartog, travelled south but were deterred by hostile coasts and Aborigines.
1770	On 29th April Captain James Cook landed near what is now Sydney and claimed the land for Britain. He reported that it was fit for colonisation.
1788	20th January, Botany Bay. The First Fleet landed seven hundred and fifty convicts to start a settlement. Persecution by settlers and European diseases greatly reduced the numbers of Aborigines.
1850	Britain gradually stopped sending convicts. Immigrants began to flood in.
1860	Within the next twenty years the population increased to over a million.
1901	The colonies agree to become a federation.
1927	The federal capital was moved from Melbourne to Canberra.
1931	Britain gave Australia the right to make their own foreign policies.
1939	Australia sent men to fight in World War II.
1942	Japan raids Darwin.
1950	Economy begins to boom.
1973	Sydney Opera House opened.
1970-1990s	Creative arts continue to be given much support. Aboriginal art is being greatly encouraged.

1. This painting could represent many things; the sun, rivers, and water journeys.
   What do you think it could represent? Discuss this with the group.

2. Lines and spots are traditional patterns used by Aborigine artists. Compare this picture with one drawn by Mondrian also using lines. Discuss them. Which do you prefer?

3. The traditional colours used are brown, red, yellow, black and white, all of which could be made from natural materials.
   What kind of materials do you think could be used to give these colours?

4. The aborigine legends and folk-lore were passed on by word of mouth and as they had no written language, much has been lost. They created a world in which animals talked, hunted and lived like men. Think of some of the cartoon animals you know that talk!

Bush Potato Dreaming.
Acrylic paint on canvas, from Yeundumu in the Western Desert area of Australia's Northern Territory, 1986.
145 cm x 94 cm.
Museum of Mankind, London.

── *TECHNIQUES* ──

This is a modern painting produced by using acrylic paint (a modern material) on canvas. However, the motifs used reflect the Aboriginal concern for their land and origins.

ACTIVITIES

Individuals

1. The boomerang is the aboriginal weapon that most people have heard of. The shape is drawn for you. If possible make a wooden boomerang, smooth all the edges and decorate it with traditional line and spot patterns and animals. If wood is not available make the boomerang from stiff card.

2. These are a few of the animal, fish and bird designs used by the Aborigines. Use these plus traditional patterns to produce a painting about animals fleeing from a bush fire. The colours to be used are red, yellow, brown, black and white.

In Small Groups

3. Choose a nursery rhyme or short children's story and change the characters to animals. Draw and paint a scene from the story.

4. Make the animals from clay. Roll out the clay to a 1.5 cm thickness. Cut out the animal shape and decorate it by pressing patterns into it. When hard, paint and varnish it.

Group or Whole Class

5. Discuss and write a story based on, "How the eagle got his wings". Use animals, birds, etc. as the participants in the story. Once the story line is decided, divide it between the class for them to illustrate. When complete the story can be joined like a Mexican codex and displayed.

Background

BUSH POTATO DREAMING

The Aboriginal peoples of Australia have a deep and subtle understanding of their surroundings.

They live by hunting, fishing when possible, and gathering natural produce. They stay in small groups and travel across vast territories living off the land as they move. They have various tools and weapons including a form of throwing stick called a boomerang.

In recent years there has been a cultural revival for the Aborigines. They have re-established their presence in their traditional areas. This has been partly financed by the sale of works of art, of which this is an example.

Although modern material has been used, the design and shapes used are traditional aboriginal motifs.

Javanese Shadow Puppets

The Thunderbird

This page may be photocopied for classroom use only.

An Aztec Game

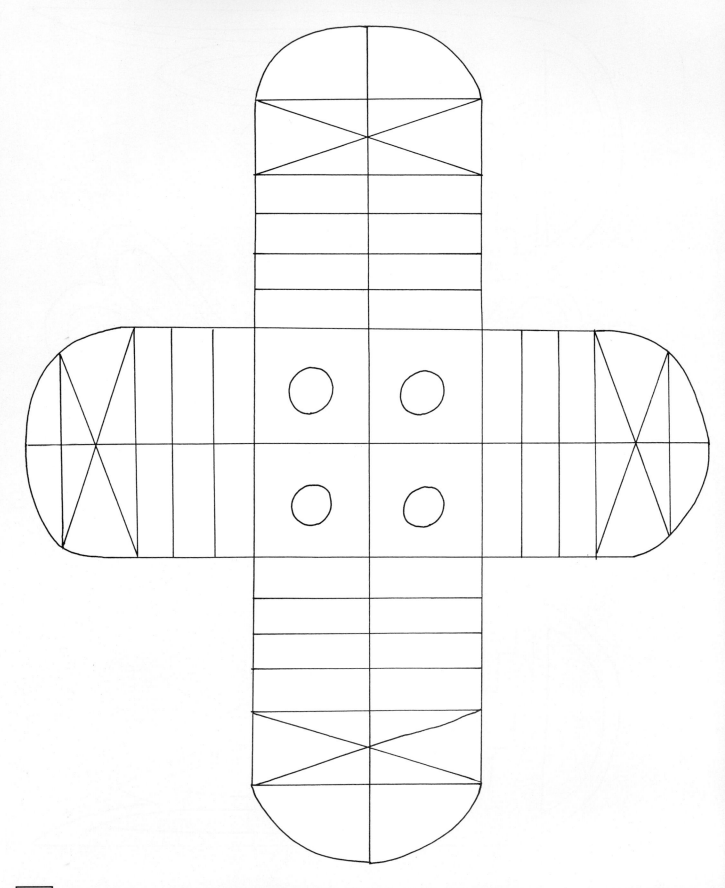

This page may be photocopied for classroom use only.

A Boomerang

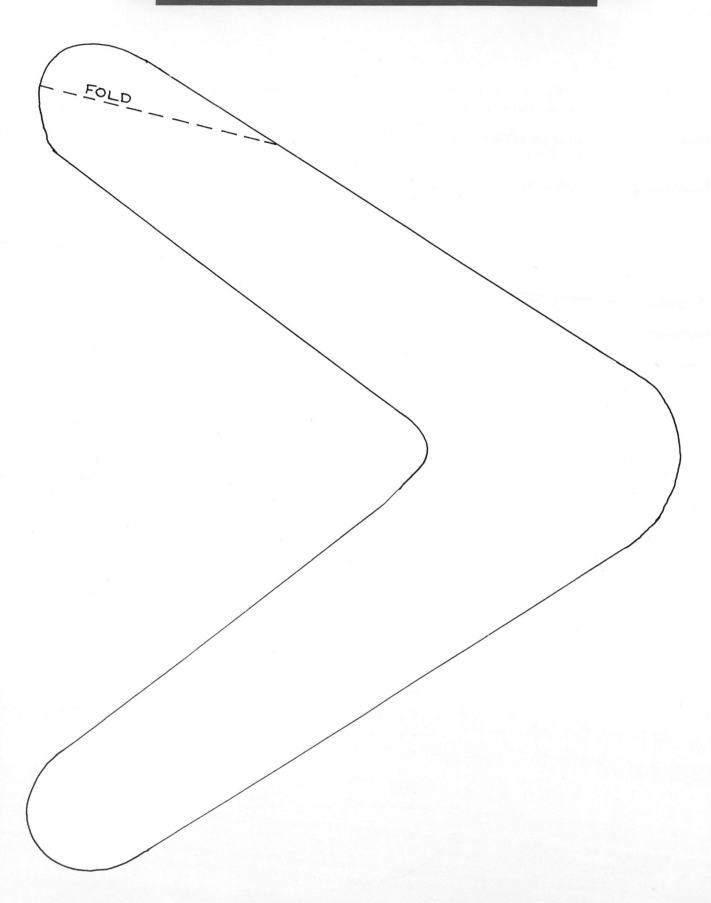

FOLD

Glossary

Aborigine Literally the first or earliest inhabitants of a country most often used with reference to Australian aborigines.

Benin A country in West Africa well known for the fine artwork in bronze and ivory that is produced.

Boomerang A native Australian curved weapon that can be thrown so that it returns to the thrower.

Codex A manuscript book used by the Aztecs in which symbols were used.

Dalang A performer, the puppeteer for Malaysian shadow puppet plays.

Dragon A fire-breathing mythical monster.

Gamelan An Indonesian musical instrument, of a type similar to a xylophone.

Hide An animal's skin, raw or dressed.

Ivory A white substance of which elephant's tusks are formed.

Lama Tibetan or Mongolian Buddhist priest.

Llasa The capital of Tibet, one of the world's most remote cities. It contains the Potala Palace, once the winter residence of the Dalai Lama, head of the Lamaist religion.

Mother-of-pearl The smooth, shiny lining of oyster and other shells.